BEYOND THE HORIZON

"IMAGINATION OF INFINITE".

SRI CHAITANYA GLOBAL SCHOOL | BHUBANESWAR

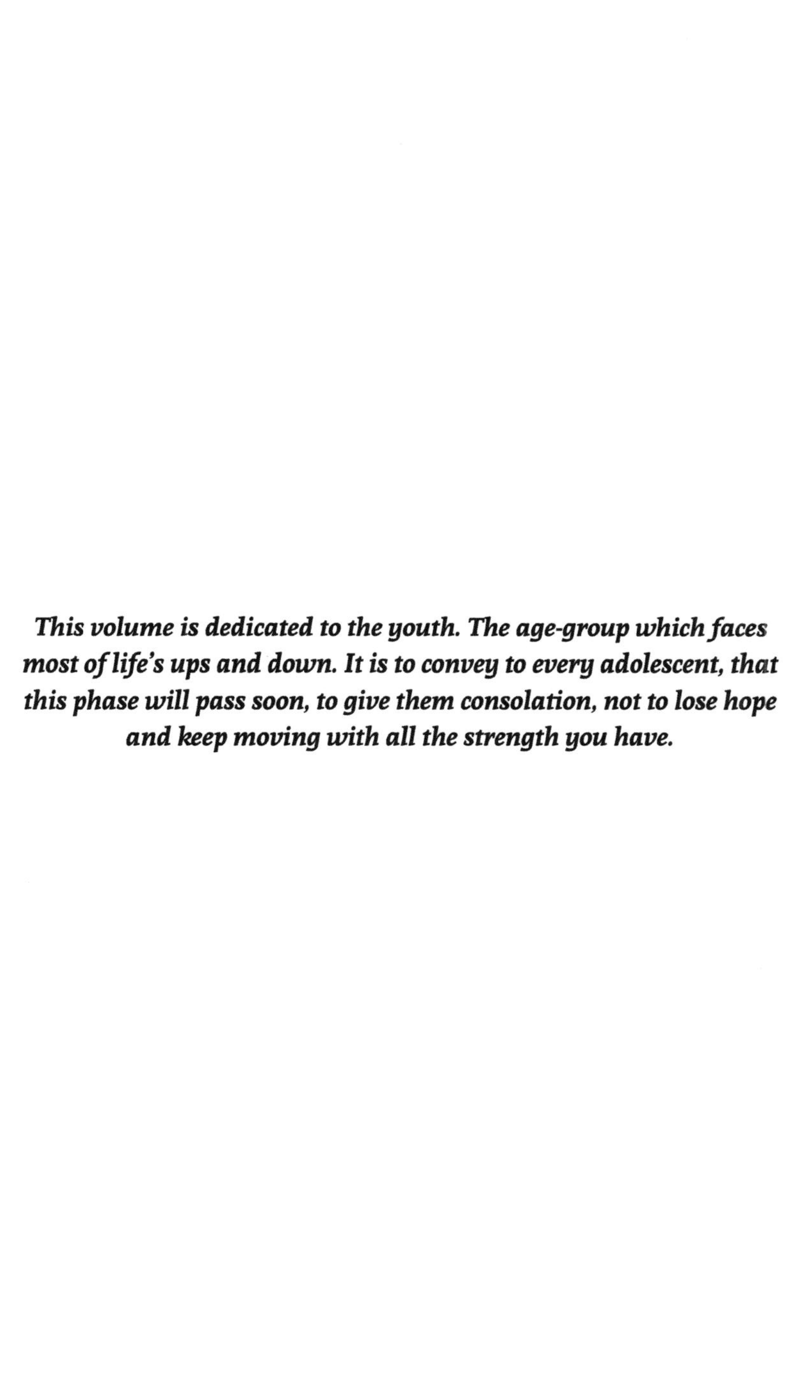

This volume is dedicated to the youth. The age-group which faces most of life's ups and down. It is to convey to every adolescent, that this phase will pass soon, to give them consolation, not to lose hope and keep moving with all the strength you have.

Contents

Contents

FOREWORD

DR. SASANKA SEKHAR KANUNGO (DIRECTOR CUM PRINCIPAL)

Absolutely it's incredible that the team has defined their talents through ballad, bullets instead. It's a fact that the book is in the pain that the team declared by representing their practical wisdom. We express our blossom of thanks to the entire young chaps for their elegant efforts and energetic Endeavour. We extend my salute to prof. *(Dr.) S.S. Kanungo* for his outstanding ideas . It's an immense pleasure for the learning opportunities have been printed by the team.

All impossible have been transferred into possible only for education. It is the fond store of activities. A nation can be succeed to stand by its own prosperity because of good education. The vivid design completion of the work couldn't have been accomplished without those chaps. They have kept the countless timings during the hectic schedule shall never be wasted. The cooperation and coordination signifies the reality among the little minds are much appreciated and duly noted.

In the *Sai Chaitanya* the nectar spreads and recollected a handful of golden seeds from the smiling lips. In a very moment I myself concepts the supreme feelings with divine soul. Love and live in love is the fundamental ingredients of the sagacity.

Acknowledgements

This work would not have been possible without the dedication and support from lovable Director cum Principal Prof. (Dr.) Sasanka Sekhar Kanungo, who has been supportive for the career goals of the students and who worked actively to provide the students with the protected academic time to pursue the goals of the students. And the institution especially indebted to Bibhuti Bhusana, Chairman of the story mirror, and all the members of SCGH. The institute is grateful to all of those with whom it has had the pleasure to work during this and other academic related works. Each of the members of the publication Committee of the Sri Chaitanya Global School, Tomando, Bhubaneswar have provided extensive personal and professional guidance and taught a great deal about both scientific research and life in general. The institute would especially like to thank all the teachers. They have taught the students more than they could would have given credit for here. Most importantly, I wish to thank the student members Jyoti Ranjan Sahoo,..... ...., who provide unending support to publish the book.

I

BIOG 1- PROF. BANI PRASAD MALI

The cardboard tells me how the days gone by, when we hold the hands of lovable heart of our family, all three stood still to smile through the hair at the camera, a sweet face of my mother which appears to have changed . It reminds the periphery we born and grown up with, it expresses the diversity and the rich heritage of the country, and it entitles to the affinity and association with the

society for a long period of time with notion.

People used to call me Bani but now Sir/Mr. is being added. Personality, ideology and prospective are changing with each passing day. Currently reading books and teaching become passion and profession; it looks as if it is inherited and explicit. In the class get mental accomplishment by making the content and concept lucid. Out of the class struggling for the utopian society by annihilating the existing social taboo in the ultra modern society.

Strength may have a different meaning for others, but strength is to ignite the unlit young mind, guide the unguided ones and stand with the last man of the society would be my understanding. Now a days playing cricket creates a pleasant environment in the brain as well as it helps to create positive vibe to maintain good rapport with the friends.

LISTEN TO THE SILENCE NOT TO THE LANGUAGE

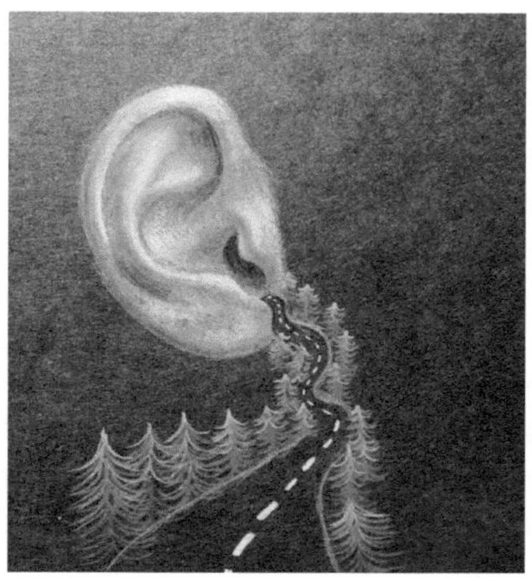

Once upon a time Buddha the light of Asia asked his followers to do a certain meditation: "Go to the society and have a look at man and female passing by, coming and going on the street. See exactly what is happening. Don't listen to their language because they are very cunning, they have become very deceptive. Listen to the meaning and if possible beyond the language and their body language."

It is hard to believe that these words are as applicable to today's modern, intellectual, word-drunken humanity as they must have been back then. The as far as my little knowledge is concerned

Buddha's teaching has more relevant for the present cunning & contradictory society. Because he is the first one in the globe who try to make us understand the meaning and importance of meditation and silence.

So the point is, look deeper into things and decode the language beyond the language to get the deeper meaning in it. People may use same words, but they don't use them with the same word with the same meaning. Listen to the meaning rather than only listening to the words. If all you listen to is the words you will never understand people. Our words come from the intellect, from the personality, which has often become so fake that we don't mean what we say. Communication has become a social etiquette it's very important in the business world; it doesn't really come from our heart or our being. Scientists tell us that words carry bio-electric energy, so the depth of meaning is proportionate to the depth of the speaker. If the speaker is a sincere and heart-oriented person, he will speak few words with profound meaning, and convey everything through his body language, his eyes, and his warmth and through facial expressions. You will be naturally drawn to this person.

This will be very helpful for your own inner growth and observing your own change in your life. Just observe people. Psychologists say it is easier as well as natural to watch people than to watch yourself, in the beginning, because people are more objective, and there is a little distance between you and them. And you can be more objective about people because you are not involved in them. Just watch. When somebody is saying something, listen to his face, to his eyes, to his being, to the gestures, and very importantly his silence and you will be simply surprised how, up to now, you have lived only with words. A person may be smiling with his lips and his eyes may be ridiculing you, rejecting you. A person may be saying 'Hello' and

holding your hand, and his whole being may be condemning you. A person may be saying, 'I love you' and his eyes may be simply denying it.

This is the language behind the language. Let everybody who comes to you be an experiment in awareness. Then, by and by, you will be able to watch yourself. Direct the entire flood of your own life energy upon yourself; and try the same technique – when you say to somebody 'I love you', listen to what you really are saying, not just to these words. Words are almost always fake. Language is very tricky and can clothe things so beautifully that the container becomes very important and you lose sight of the content. People have become very sophisticated as far as their surface is concerned, yet their innermost core remains primitive. Listen to the centre of the circumference. If you are silent within, you can go into the words like an X-ray, and suddenly you feel a deep wellbeing arising in you, a deep joy for no apparent reason.

II

BIOG 2- PRIYANKA BAG

"Work that much hard that one day your signature will become an autpograph"- *TIM* NOTKE

The word 'a servant' of the society always makes her active in the wrestle of life. Being an undergraduate with a tumultuous voice- " The great endearing Priyanka with a heavy load of emotion" in the voyage span of SCGs to do some incantation in life

like a illimitable ether. While spoting the orb on bench, she just make it round. The hunch attain in her intellect, Wow! She traveled the whole world. In the obscurity of life, always an aspiration to tang new professionalism to explore her boast fortune. We edificate one thing from the clock "an endless process" it stimulates her towards the reasoning of supersticious but- She must applaud it without fear. Apart of all the shining, there a silence exist, a dark lonely part of which petrify the face. As a kiddy from a hamlet she is filled with lots of notion to be distinctive and ingenious like a milestone.

A SCHOLASTIC TEENAGER

" I am standing here today with my voice. My voice which not only speaks for my designation, but also for the struggle faced during the journey. My well- wishers, let me inform you not much about failure, my victories, rather more tales of my dedication and patience would be an inspiration. Each and everything which added up beneath my feet to make me stand here."

" Lightest like a day, darkest like a night

difference of point in both the sight".

" Hard work determines but smart work facilitate,

no teen is perfect if they don't have any effect."

So, my story starts from a small village, where certain groups inhibited. In a cloudy sky of August, a joint family of around

veintemembers were hoping for a girl child. By the grace of god and blessings, I was born as the first daughter in my family. My father's love has been just unmatched and un-paralleled, he marked a charm on my face and envisage his dreams to be fulfilled by me. I grew up in a family with a political background because of which, from the very early stage I have gained interest to listen to problems of others and wondering about some possible solutions. Since childhood I had never argued or disturbed my parents for the school works and I used to managed a few house chores like cooking, dressing up myself etc.

Voice- a God's gift. It surprises me how someone can crack a joke even at it. I got to know about it, when I took part in a song competition. The judges and the audience seated there started laughing at me. It shocked me, I asked one of my friends.

"Why all of them were laughing at me?"

He giggled and answered- "Have you ever listened to your own voice? How roughly you vocalize, you are not capable of becoming a singer, when you talks it seems as if you are shouting".

Is that why you all laughed at me always?

With a hilarious laugh "no, no! don't be sad you may become a great loudspeaker in future"- he joked.

I have a terrible voice, still it had played an important role while leading a group which no one could. During march past, I greatly handled every situation. I made a promise to myself that, those who had laughed at me, in future would queue to buy tickets just to hear me.

I struggled a lot for my voice and was in a hope that- in future I would shut their mouth up. The very next day, they again tries to bully me regarding body shaming as I was a chubby, fatty girl, not having a perfect body shape, no dresses fits me..bla...bla...

Not able to concentrate on studies, these words were grooving in my intellect, and that's why I scored less percentage. Not just mentally, it pressurized me physically too.

" In this way you are getting prepared for your board exam? Why are you marks degrading all of a sudden?

I didn't know how to reveal the truth in front of them and has left always speechless.

Admiring at my face my parents without uttering a word went away. In night, not being able to control my emotions anymore. I went to my mother to express my feelings what exactly happens with me that leads to my low percentage.

After hearing all my problems she advised me that- "life is not a straight path, not a zig-zag, it's a curious one with a critical, mysterious and incomprehensible problems. By facing problems would make us capable of learning new things about the world", so not to petrify, just face it.

"Thank you mom, your word consoled me". Paying attention to my mom's words and the emotion I motivated myself how to leave behind the thoughts of the world.

The next day when I went to the school, they bullied me again, but holding the words of my mother in my mind, I ignored them with a pretty smile. This continued for a long period of time and in return I gave them a smile. Humanity finally struck them when my hardwork and determination made me the " TOPPER" of my class.

I changed the mindset of my friends but, I didn't know how to change the mentality of the society in which we all live in, where people judge everyone by the intimacy and intention of a teen. On the other hand, as a kiddy while I returned back to home from the school with my male friends, the people around me looked weirdly towards us, as if I was doing a crime, not only this some of our other works were also being judged. So this thinking of the society should be avoided by everyone.

Negativity is necessary. Because without having it, you would never try getting over it. That's how the life challenges you to overcome negativity. So philandering from the society, I, with a tumulteous voice as an IAS officer in front of you holding a degree of sucess in my hand.

Applauses..... Applauses

Drawing of a ladder on a plane sheet of paper, tried to inform you about the unforeseeable future."A prolix mind and a gifted mind", determine the condition of a teenager. Not all are capable ,some are also uncapable.Its the period of time where hormonal imbalance, puberty, the growth of body parts occur. Some get teased while some are praised but we must always be ready to raise. Peer pressure, stress, bullying, anxiety, autism knock the doors , your confidence never create any disorder. Not so hot , not so cool, be positive when anyone scolds. Respect the elder in return you get the boon. Follow the right way which helps you to achieve your dreamy success.

III

BIOG 3- ANKITA BEHERA

"If you can't figure out your purpose,
figure out your passion, for your passion will lead you right into your purpose".
by- BISHOP T.D JAKES

In this contemporary world of race, she wants to move forward leaving her past behind. She holds the desire to proceed

on a path that was left untouched. It's really bizarre but she wants to fire. She dares to make the difference that remains unexpected. Inspired by the nature poet, Robert Frost, a girl like the wallflower finally craves to spill her heart's wishes 'ANKITA' of SCGs, the ardent one who loves to spent most of her time alone, experimenting dynamics of her life. Thrillers fascinate her with their unique style of mysterious tales filled with suspense. The beauty of multiple languages ignites her with numerous designs. Her grandfather is the greatest motivator who supports and guide, giving her many ethical values. To see her family with a bright smile of satisfaction is the greatest urge buried deep in her heart.

I WAS'NT UGLY, BUT I DIDN'T CONSIDER MYSELF BEAUTIFUL.

Late winter morning, with dizzling rain falling on the window pane. I was sitting on my bed holding up a cup of coffee, spending time watching the beautiful scenery outside. The shining droplets on the leaves,the smell of petrichor, the sound of the rain falling on the tin roof was mismerizing. After spending some time gazing there, suddenly my doorbell rang. I walked towards the door, thinking about who was at the door in these hours of rain when no one knew where I lived. In a small cottage at the top of the hill. There was an old man standing outside the door holding a bunch of beautiful post cards. I brought those

letters and thanked him for his hard work. I offered him to stay until the rain stops but he refused and hurriedly went to deliver the letters. I took the letters inside and started reading them one by one.

The colourful letters were decorated by the children with their creative minds all engrossed in the small postcards. There were plenty of letters but my eyes went to one of the cards painted black and a girl sketched covering her face with a scarlett scarf. It was written " The beauty of my village" on the top of the letter. I wondered what was inside while tearing the edge of the letter. There was a poem written by Anne.

She usually writes short eye-catching poems and sends them every Sunday. She describes nature and puts in a lot of effort. Her unique thoughts will motivate you to write a poem on your own.

But this time she wrote,"Mam, every time I wrote about nature, but today I tried something new. I decided to write a poem describing myself and the things have occurred to me in the past few years. I would like you to read my letter and advise me..." She illustrated the way society treats her. From the time of existence in the world, people called her an ugly girl and few criticized her mother for giving birth. They suggested Anne's mother to abort the child but she didn't agree. They even insisted that the child is ugly so, she should throw her in the garbage, but she decided to leave the neighborhood instead. When she got her husband's support, they decided to go far from the city. They went to a small village where the people were nice and helped her to get rid of the miserable situation and even let her live until Anne made herself capable. Now that she has crossed eighteen and has a permanent job in the nearby town. She decided to take her parents but the way she got closer to the villagers, made a part of her heart empty. She then describes the way her father had gone through to educate her in a big international school. Her friends thought her ugly and few of them got scared of get close to her.

During her teenage years, when she was in her adolescence stage, she had pimples all over her face and dark circles under her eyes. So, her seniors as well as her classmates bullied her and a few of them even criticized her parents. But she decided to stand brave and fight because of her parents' struggle. Soon after his father got to know, he took a strong decision to change the school. Their lives became more miserable, but regardless, the villagers laid a helping hand. They asked her to go to college to complete her education and paid the rest of the fees for her.

Now she is thankful to them. Just words can't describe the feelings deep inside her heart. She decides to pay them all a small tribute with this marvellous poem. Concluding the difference between the thinking processes of the two societies belonging to the same 'The Mother Earth'. She wanted to seek my advice to motivate her and give some ideas for a Thanksgiving party to the villagers as well as her parents, especially her father, who devoted all his life to making her girl independent in all respective. She even told me that she is taking the responsibility for taking care of her gracious mother and to guide and teach her little sibling the ethics that her father taught.

My eyes teared up after reading the poem and the letter. I began to wonder if I could ever meet her. I responded to the letter and requested to visit the girl who inspired me with her great thoughts. Sitting on a rocking chair, yet I keep thinking about Anne, " The prettiest girl by heart". She changed my perspective with a single poem. That day I realised, " I wasn't ugly, but I didn't consider myself beautiful".

MY INNER SOUL- VERSE 1

What constitutes the word beauty?
Is it the thing which brings good essence;
Or is it something which people judge by our face?

Do I look beautiful? I ask when I make-up.
The answer I got always "Ugh! You ugly girl, Shut up!"

The more I asked the sadder I got.
And at those times, I had no one who could have fought.

But why do I need opinions of them?
While questioning myself my head bowed in shame.

Self love is something which I have never done
Why have I considered myself a burden?

I would love myself I committed to me
It shouldn't matter what says he or she
I got the answer eventually for the question asked.
Beauty is in the inner me when I am unmarked.

IV

BIOG 4- SANIDHYA DAS

Yet , 3k weeks left in your life ! Sounds huge right ? To him as well. This fair guy with seriousness in his mind is basically a 12th grader. With all the love and affection for his mother, is a person with some of the most savage came back for everything you speak on a random basis. With an ambition to peripatetic around the globe as a sailor dressed in white via the sea ways; treading goods

over a nations to others. Oh wait ! Airways and land ways would be the one he'd select for a vacation. Swimming through the clear blue sea of Maldives has been a constant dream since ages. An aromatic pot of mughlai cuisine is all it takes to reserve a place in his heart. An introvert, with the best choice of words after a few months of acquaintance, Sanidhya would never fail to amuse you with his secret talents.

THE JOY OF YOUTH SPORTS

"I can't be a trash forever."

This is the fourth time we both had secured the lowest marks in the class.

"Hey! Hiki, How's your day going" Nagato asked in a casual manner.

"I think good, but don't know what is going on, in my dad's mind." No one will be satisfied after getting lowest marks in the class, my mind prompted this.

"Hiki, come here " Dad called me calmly.

"How much have you scored this time?"

"30...." I murmured, I was scared because last time he became mad due to my low marks.

"Hmm..., not much better than before, I think son you should be more grievous towards your studies. You don't know the world is a dump yard of wicked people. The only thing that you have to do is to get out of your comfort zone, only then you can change, grow up and transform."

"Yes dad!" I said in an inspired tone. Dad's words always manage to motivates me.

"Ok... Just be true to your words, I am trying to find a good mentor who will come and teach you at home" Dad said seriously in an intimating voice.

After several attempts for a mentor, Nagato's Dad followed the same, that my father had thought of "Getting a mentor." We tried the best to excel in studies and finally the examination date arrived.

"Yo Hiki ! How much have you scored this time?" asked Nagato. The exams were wrapped up by then, and he asked me in a happy tone may be he had scored better marks than me.

"33%..., ha ha, what about you?"I said with a smirk on my face. At that moment I was being diverted by the thought of my father's reaction to the marks I have secured.

"Whooh! We the spitting image of each other" he said laughingly.

I think we are the best buddies in the world, irrespective of what comes we won't change ever.

"Am I happy of this? Hell nah! I am not"

"How much have you scored this time son?" Dad asked.

Shit! How am I going to look into my father's eyes? Whatever he had done for me is unmatched, but I am of no worth. It was totally contrary in the case of Nagato's Dad, he never cared about how much his son was scoring as he earned in millions.

"33%..." Said bluntly. I was horrified what was going to happen in my ridiculous life.

"33%? You have improved a bit, but, aren't these the still the lowest marks in the class?" Dad asked roughly.

"Yes they are", mumbled slowly.

"What have you been doing all this time? Huuh! I arranged a mentor for you because your time was being wasted while cycling to such a distance and you are not improving at all" he shouted out loud. I was being frightened.

"Sorry Dad" my eyes were full of tears. I didn't know what I was supposed to do.

"What sorry? Your sorry isn't going to get you marks and what are you thinking if you will study well and you will get a nice job, will it benefit me? Not at all, it will be for your own future." he shouted.

"Yes..." I mumbled.

"I don't have so much of money to waste on you, now you have to go to your mentor by cycling, he is not coming home anymore and it can be considered as a workout as well, you are looking lethargic nowadays." he said normally.

"Ok Dad" I replied.

Then I started going to my tuition by a cycle. But Nagato was still having his home tutoring. By the way, I had started enjoying cycling daily. It mad me more energetic and happy. The exams were knocking at the door and I wasn't prepared for it at all but I am going to give my best.

"Hiki-Hiki! I improved I got 36%, better than before and Dad said he is going to get me a present" Nagato said with a big smile on his face.

"Ohh! I got 40%", it was a creepy smile from me though, I was kind of happy for getting better marks than before but I knew, these were still not enough to make my Dad happy.

"So, Hiki how much this time?" Dad asked with a confused expression. I thought he was serious this time but I was sure I'd slip away as I had secured better marks than Nagato.

"40%, it is better than before right? I got better marks than Nagato also", I informed with a huge grin. I was sure that I was going to be safe this time.

"40% mmm, it is the highest marks you have secured, I think. But how can you call it better? And from where have you learnt comparing yourself with others? Huh! You all are going to the same school, reading the same books and even being taught by the same teachers, then why are they scoring good marks, not you? There is still some time to make yourself improved, so better be serious, I am not going to tell you every time", he explained me with a serious face.

I knew that was hard for me but I was able to give the best. I asked one of my closest teacher for ideas to improve my studies and he suggested me to join yoga classes for mental peace and concentration enhancement. I joined the school yoga classes but I bunked the first three classes in a row. Nothing to worry about, RIGHT? But on the fourth day I thought of trying it once and I felt better. It amazed me. Then I started going to the yoga classes regularly and also started accompanying my dad during his morning walks. I also tried other sports, it made me energetic and I developed my body skills with each passing days. I also enjoyed them. I felt like I was improving every day. I was excited for my upcoming annual sports. I and Nagato used to came first in the annual sports every year and this time it would be more fun. The pre-annual sports begun at our school. I performed pretty well, in spite I performed better than Nagato and Nagato was sort of shocked. Seeing this, I challenged him to compete with me in the annual sports. The day of annual sports arrived, everything was going pretty smooth, I performed far better than Nagato.

"Woo-hoo!" I scored 101* in the interschool match and everyone was cheering for me, that feeling was insane. But god's plans were not in my favor and I fell... It was 100meter sprint, the ligament of my right knee was torn and I thought this was the end of my career in sports. While leaving the ground I heard the laughter of Nagato and some of his friends.

"Yo Hiki! How's your day going? You don't look good though, He-he! Do one thing, don't fly much high you aren't allowed to be better than Me." he said with a nasty look , later I got to know that Nagato had gathered people to defeat me in the annual sports. As he was not able to defeat me, he made arrangements to make me trip over and fall it was devastating. I could not get this incident out of my mind and this incident influenced my whole life.

Years passed........

"And the best council awards for sports goes to, Mr. Hiki Hyodo, who also has built a school for students to enjoy the sports in their daily life and is able to create their career in sports ground. He has been rewarded with a sum of Rs 5, 00,000 " declares the judge. Nagato was watching television and this award function caught his sight. His face dropped, the company he had inherited from his father faced a bankrupt. He was sitting with no job. His savings were getting over day by day and he didn't have any other idea to earn his living.

His KARMA played its role well leaving him on the FLOOR

"Life is very similar to a boxing ring. Defeat is not declared, when you fall down it is declared when you refuse to rise up."- *By A.P.J Abdul Kalam.*

V

BIOG 5- AKLESH KUMAR PANDA

The hana of instigating colonist vocalize desire of contradictory sub -thinking named "AKLESH PANDA" can unbolt precisely as well as condidly the staggering power of language by

going through the romantism of belles-letters. The lad imaginative to the chunk of note paper can demonstrate a mansion for the enhancement of the human kind.The desire of being a heart failure neonatal cardiologist has always waken me from the intense drowse. Not only this what I desire for, the torn yellow pages of the "Harry Potter" had always fizzed my capillaries of the cerebellum. As an infant I had always been impelled in relation to the graphics globe of "Marvel Studios." The essence of being a scholar of SCGs had a great experience for me till age.

I WAS BORN INTELLIGENT BUT RESERVATION RUINED ME.

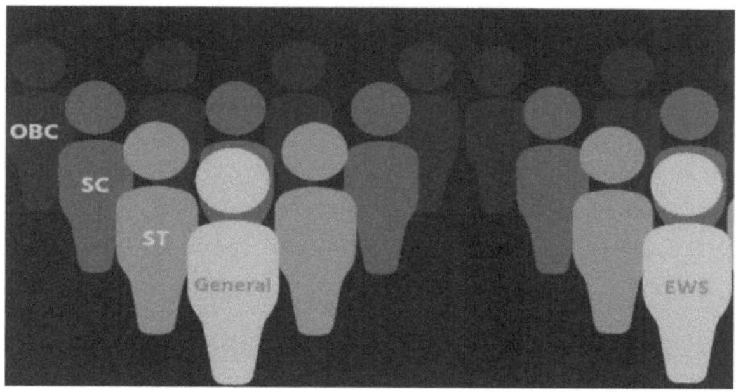

It is a foggy morning and a miserable news knock's my door that my friend Rahul has left us. He has committed suicide with no reason found till now. I have to go to my friend's funeral. After completion of the last rite his parent invited me to their home, I was having so uneasy feelings, it was not a good feeling at all. When I got to his room, at the corner of the self I found a personal dairy named "I was born intelligent but reservation ruined me" and when I started turning those pages it was the life history of my friend.

In the book it was explained that how he always secure good mark in the examination but because of reservation in examination he didn't got admission into any institution and all his hard work went in vain where as one of his friend named Ranjit who belongs to reserve category got admission into the

reputed medical institution even if he has scored very low marks.

When I went into the diary, I found the story of two friends Rahul and Ranjit.

Rahul a studious boy who always scores good mark in all examination from his childhood and Ranjit who is not so good in studies was his friend. They were friends from childhood.

Rahul always work hard and always secures above 90 percentage Ranjit who does not care about studies gets 40 percentage who barely passes any exams. Facing up and down in studies Rahul, is still a friend of Ranjit and moreover supports him a lot in in his studies.

As days were passing by, they became older and the time came when they joined a collage and later get to know about competition. He worked with his friend day and night for board exams and both pass the board examination. One by 90 percentage and another by 50 percentages, the both were happy after seeing their mark. After completion of the board examination Rahul was told by his father to join coaching because as they belong to general category he have to score more mark in the entrance examination. So thereafter his father send him to Kota for two years of coaching. This news also went to Ranjit but he was not interested to go in such type of coaching institution. He was thinking to work in his But he was scolded by his father and asked to join a coaching institute. But he explained his dad "Dad you know how my situation is, I am not good at all in studies" but his father told him that they belong to reserved category due to which he should not have to worry about marks.

They just have to score 40 percentage to pass the entrance examination by passing such examination he can become doctor and earn so much money which can be even more then his business, after hearing all these from his father he agreed to join a coaching and requested his father to let him join the coaching institute, where Rahul was studing.

When Ranjit also joined the coaching institution Rahul became so much happy and became charged. They both started studying together, worked hard together, Rahul also suggested him some tricks that would help him to score better marks. Later Ranjit was loosing his confidence on himself so, Rahul tried his best to help him he went through all the previous year questions he can gather and choose out the question which could be important or can be repeated this year also and built up confidence in Ranjit. The time of the entrance examination has came near, they both were working hard day and night for the entrance examination, which will change their life.

Ranjit took all the possible help from Rahul and secured 450 and passed and got a good government medical college , while Rahul in other hand worked day and night to achieve his goal got 600 mark but did not got a government medical college due to his caste was general. He went down to depression because he was good student and also after getting good result he was not able to get a government college.

He could not handle that much of depression and eventually choose the path of suicide.

"Here I completed reading the dairy of my friend"

After reading the story tear came out of my eyes and I can’t hold my feeling anymore.

I went back home and started writing about reservation. And I want to convey a message to the society about the dark part of reservation.

Reservation is all about:

1. Reservation is just a priviledge not a fundamental right "you cannot build up anything on the foundation of caste, you cannot build up a nation, you cannot build up a morality.- "Dr. B.R.Ambedkar".

2. The entire fault lies in the practise of reservation based on caste that our country is a victim.

In my opinion:

1. The reservation system in India, began to help people, has started a war among people of lower cast and people of higher caste.

2. Reservation system should be taken out from India besause if our nation is one, our society is one , our school is one, than why should a ST/SC caste people get more benefit than a General.

3. God have given the same brain to every human, also teacher are teaching the same thing to both reserved and non- reserved caste people then why by getting less mark they get a good position and a General caste people after hard working day and night is not getting a proper position

Surely a time will come when there will be a war between reserved and non-reserved category.

At last i want to say that,

By writting this story with a small opinion of mine, I want to convey the country about the dark sights of "RESERVATION SYSTEM."

VI

BIOG 6- ANURAG PANDA

Its deep dark with the world surrounded which produces an echo of falling drops of water from the sky, walking alone on the

street, with a sudden look to the glass, shows the reflection of "ANURAG." Pain and grief came to his life but a bunch of books make it delight. Having an ambition of getting better than what he was before, working day and night to give himself a better role with having red and black on him, roams the street for having a search of something which was never been seen. The path of life is filled with flower and thrones to choose out of thrones, he used the spectacles called "SCGS"Its deep dark with the world surrounded which produces an echo of falling drops of water from the sky, walking alone on the street, with a sudden look to the glass, shows the reflection of "ANURAG." Pain and grief came to his life but a bunch of books make it delight. Having an ambition of getting better than what he was before, working day and night to give himself a better role with having red and black on him, roams the street for having a search of something which was never been seen. The path of life is filled with flower and thrones to choose out of thrones, he used the spectacles called "SCGS"

NEPOTISM- A BOON FOR ONE AND BANE FOR ANOTHER.

In this humongous world there are innumerous people, where some are good and some are bad. Here some utilize their power and position for their own benefits, and don't even bother for others.

A beautiful city "Pataliputra" is the old name of "Patna". In this positive place there were many cheap minded people, out of them "Lingraj Tripathy"was a powerful politician who was elected as the "Excise Minister" of Bihar. But he was a bit softer hearted towards his son. The name of his son was "Bhawani Tripathy". Although born like an ordinary child yet he was always served like a prince since his child hood. He took admission in "Godwin International School", one of the

renowned schools of the city. Although Bhawani was a weak student but he was vibing like a gangster in the school. He was bullying, harassing, ragging, and torturing other students. He had a best friend namely "Baliar Singh." Baliar Singh was son of a most wanted criminal "Dhruva Bhai." One day they both argued and had a fight with teachers, so the teacher gave complain to the principal. But instead the principal kicked the teacher out of the school, who complained about Baliar Singh and Bhawani.

Since then every teacher, student and non-teaching staffs were afraid of both of them. There was a pretty girl namely "Mehak Agarwal." She was gorgeous and elegant as well as stylish. Bhawani and Baliar both had a crush on her. They both tried a lot to knock into eyes of her. At last Baliar successfully impressed Mehak. Bhawani was offended by Baliar Singh and was envious from their relationship. So Bhawani decided to create misunderstanding between them, but he failed to do so. But he was not able to do so and that thought of Baliar and Mehak together made him reach his trigger point, so he planned to kill his buddy.

On the darkest night of February that was 12on the calendar he called Baliar for Cocktail party, but his intentions were something else. He added some heavy narcotic materials in the drink of Baliar that made Baliar feel fuzzy and he dropped down on the floor. Then seeing this Mehek was anxious and worried about the situation and the people present there also got worried.

Than Bhawani with a glass of whisky in right hand and a Desert Eagle in left hand approached towards Baliar who was laying almost unconscious on the floor then he pointed his gun on the forehead of Baliar and the last words of Baliar were "Foolish my

father will burn you alive!" Hearing this he fired the gun. Bloods covered the floor with some scrap of skull. Seeing this Mehak fall on the floor and got unconscious.

The last word of Baliar raged him up. He took his car and slammed it in front of the door of Dhruva house and kicked the door wide opened then fired some random bullets. After some time he returned to his car with his hands soaked in blood then he looked back to the wife of Dhruva and said "Your son was talking about his father... Here I am standing in front of you after sending both his father and his father's father to the hell!!! Remember me I am Bhawani who erased your 3 generations in a single night!!!!...."

One week passed, but there was no outcome of her FIR that she had filed against Bhawani. She sat in front of the police station and screamed "This is unfair the police is acting like PUPPET by the hands of the politicians and powerful people.... The LAW IS IN THE HANDS OF CRIMINALS!!"

Seeing this a man also supported her and said

"It shows the crucial, nasty and dark part of nepotism!"

With this it was clear that the powerful people were manipulating the law and system for their own benefits . The next story shows how a young talented man lost his job due to Bhawani own will :-

A hard working boy named "Pranit." He was putting all his efforts day and night to reach his goal. He got an appointment for a job for which he shifted to Patna. But in other hand Bhawani wants a job, both of them applied for the same one. But the application of "Pranit" was denied but the application of Bhawani was accepted that made "Pranit" shocked. He

complained this to the *Human Rights Office* but they didn't help him. This news was heard by Bhawani then Bhawani mad out and kidnapped Pranit and scared him to leave the job expectation the veins. This news got viral throughout the state and a 3-stard Police from Jujharpur stood up for helping Pranit to retain his job and to punish the evil. He was Pathak baba he was of 32 years with a lot of experience and 4 encounters in a streak. He was a dedicated, respectful, and a polite officer. As no one was willing to help Pranit, Pathak baba takes his side and took the oath to punish Bhawani. Even after the warning given by Bhawani to Pranit, he went to the police station and again filed a FIR against him. So Bhawani became more serious and furious, against Pranit. Past ago Pathak Baba had killed Debraj Tripathy the brother of Lingraj Tripathy while trying to encounter Bhawani. So Bhawani was holding some personal issues with Pathak Baba. After seeing both Pranit and Pathak baba working as a team to defeat him he killed both Pathak baba and Pranit. He sent the dead body of Pranit to his home town in a cartoon tore his every body part into pieces and put a stamp on it with the address of Mirzapur!!.. The body of Pathak Baba was hanged in front of his own house with a message written on it "I am The GOD OF MY OWN WORLD!!"

Here in this part we saw how cruel was Bhawani and his misuse of power against common people.

NO MATTER HOW MUCH YOU WORK HARD OR EDUCATED IF POLITICIAN POWER WAS THERE YOUR SUCCES WILL BE SNACHED BY THEM. Nepotism of this politician has gone far beyond the limits now, Bhawani has started corrupting others land. He made his own rules and regulation which was bound to be followed by the people.

It was the village Jujhpur, which is situated 60km away from Patna. A boy named "Surya Chandra Pathak"used to live there. He was the son of great police officer Pathak Baba, who got quite famous in Pranit case. He was just 22 year old, he lost his father. The anger turned into a frustration which changed his mind set. The aim of Surya wanted to take revenge from Bhawani.

He had a best friend "Bani Babu." Who used help him in his all types of conditions. It was a chilly day both Surya and Bani were travelling in a train from Jujhpur to Muzafpura approx 70km away. When they were on the train they came face to face with the gang members of Bhawani and at first sight they attacked both of them and over numbered them. They beat them very hard and made them stay on their knee then a bridge came and seeing that "Bani told Surya to jump out to the river" but he didn't did that but suddenly Bani pushed him out and said "Good bye my Dear friend!" Next morning the newspaper showed the headline that a man was torn apart on the Rail line.

After 4 years, finally he relaxed when he heard about the election date. When both Surya and Bhawani particularly stand for their party. The aim of the Surya was to defeat Bhawani and free the people by his corruption. For the sake of vote, Surya visited every house and gave them hope of positivity, filled their need where everyone started love and being relaxed, where Bhawani showed his power of money. With many difficulties, finally he defeated Bhawani and became the mantri. This ends of the nepotism era. Bit still thought arrived in the mind Surya definitely won but,

"Is Bhawani shows his money power?" Surya with full proved planning, police raid on Bhawani house, to collect all treasure .It is not easy to found but at last he found all his black money that was forcefully corrupted by Bhawani.

Bhawani was arrested for keeping black money in his home, so he was prisoner for life time

At last, under Surya rules and regulation made everyone happy and also he fulfilled their requirement .

VII

BIOG 7- PRAKASH DAS

The one who impulse and ach for a combat should be equipped for it. Loaming in a hushed pavement with the thrum of being scouted by the one who is always in hunt of the ingenious "PRAKASH"The alluring and enthralling stars the swirling leaflet cotyledon the discreet tongue-tied scrap had guided him

up to the catbird seat that he seriously don't deserve. But still with stout-hearted bravery, and stand up in the podium like "Eren yesager" standing in the lands of Marey. He is new to the sight of literature like a newbie in the arena of the Erangle. Collecting guts and gaining experience with every battle against each words to make it a sentence. Books has always attracted him towards the innovative minds behind them (authors) and h is trying his level best to match their level of approaching and representing their thoughts on a sheet of paper. As a child he had always been attracted towards the fascinating world of comics and fictional stories. And now he is trying his luck in the stage of literature.

"THE ART OF WAR"- SPIRITUALITY FOR CONFLICT.

Here I am standing on the corpse of my own fallen comrades. Where ever I see its only blood and blood. The dead bodies are coming towards me?

Dead comrades: - "It's all because of you...."

Repeated voice: - "You deserve death......" Death!!.... Death!!...

(Dream snapped)

"Holy shit!!" Again that same thing? What's wrong with me? Why there is blood everywhere...And those dead bodies! Why they look so familiar?

Leave it... this might just be a nightmare. It's already late for school. I should get going.

"Woo-hoo" I made it in time the bus has not left yet ...

But that nightmare... Why is it distracting me? Does it have any connection with me?

So here I am Eric a simple boy living all by myself with just a boring and ordinary life. Not have many friends. Talking to people is so rubbish and time wasting. And I don't have that much time to dump. I live in a small apartment which is more than enough for a loner like me. I spent most of my times just lying on the roof of the school looking at the wide blue yonder.

The nightmares kept on coming everyday and their intensity also increased gradually. The situations became more critical that I started to see those dead bodies with my open eyes. They were rushing towards me in the bus station while returning to my apartment and suddenly I bumped with an old lady who was looking at me weirdly. The aroma is being terrible step by step.

"KNOCK" ..."KNOCK"

It might be the owner... Shit ... Shit!!! It had been two months since I paid the rent. For that he will eat me alive... he is a livid old folk who doesn't understand even a single word of anyone what a "Stubborn!!"

"Hey dumb it's me Itsuki"... "Open the damn door"

So this stupid guy in front of the door knocking is my one and only so called friend. With a very ugly face which looks like a mongoose. But he is the only soul I can trust and he knows everything about my life except for these nightmares.

I should open the door before he breaks in.

Itsuki might have come to inform me about the assignment. "Shit!!" those teachers! They will ruin my brain one day for sure. Like I said that I spend most of my times on the roof and for the sake of that I skip almost all my class and Itsuki is like an aide who saves me from every single crisis. If not him the headmaster would have kicked me out of the school far before.

(I opened the door)

Eric: - "Hey Dude!"... "What's going on?"

"Just like the typical Eric bunked the whole class and Here I the Great Itsuki who attended the class' everyday ..." Itsuki said with a proud look in his eyes.

Eric:-"Ok... Ok but didn't you remember the marks of last semester"? You had half of my total mark..."LOL......

With a smirk he changed the topic and said "Hey dude you will be really happy to know that the all waited VACCATIONS are here." "AHH-YESSS no more school, no to those painful assignments, and those teachers!!" "OHH at last for these four weeks we are free from all those curses!"

At that moment the facial expression his face was so dramatizing that I burst into laughing.

And I said "The vacations were normal for me as I used to bunk most of mine classes."

Suddenly the dead bodies appeared and I was stone cold at that moment and was not able to move even an inch.... They were all over the place grunting and rushing towards me and suddenly I heard a voice.

"ERIC!! ERIC!!"

It was itsuki who was shocked to see me standing still. Suddenly I snapped out of it and was sweating all over. He grabbed me and asked "What happened to you Bro??" "I saw you were not responding to my words, and were acting abnormally!!"

Eric:-"Nothing... Just it is something that I can't explain to you properly" "It is like I am having nightmares with my eyes wide opened"

Itsuki:-"I can see you are behaving weirdly since last week!" "You can share what's going on with me because we are best buddies; you know that I am here for you every time."

"Nah! It's nothing I can feel the presence of dead people near me and most of the time they just appear in front of me and they try to force me to die!!" I said with a very scared face.

Itsuki was confused by hearing what I have said to him but still to sympathized me and counsel me to visit my village during this vacation. And it seemed relevant to me too. I thought that visiting the village would refresh my mind and will inject some positive vibes in me. So I packed up my luggage and set out for village the next day.

It was a very long and boring journey all through the journey I was accompanied by an old guy who was talking about some ridicules facts and hearing those was so painful that my ears were almost on the stage to bleed out. I reached the railway station early in the morning and I saw my Grandpa. He was waiting for me and at that moment I was almost on my tears because I saw him after a very long and hectic period of time.

He was looking the same as I have seen him 7 years before. That same smile on his face with light beard and moustache and his hairs were still reddish just like mine. He waved his hand and hugged me. Then we went to our home and at night we cooked fish which he caught by himself from the river nearby. It was so delicious that I licked my fingers for more than an hour I think! After that delicious dinner we spend some time on the roof talking about how I am spending my city life. I talked about Itsuki to him and said how much dumb as well as helpful he is. Then after a healthy conversation we went to sleep as I had a rough journey.

Dead bodies: - "You have to die!!" "Because of you we all loosed our life ... we will drag you into the HELL!!"

I scrammed and jumped out of my bed. My grandpa rushed to my room and took me up and asked me what happened .I said him that I am scared to DIE!! Then he asked how you suppose to die? You are talking rubbish....

Then I explained him everything about those nightmare and daydreams and he was shocked too. Then he patted on my back and said it's a call from your past and also said that he has gone through this type of situation before. Then he took me to a old Monk next morning who was having a very needle pointed beard with a saffron colored robe. My grandpa explained everything to him and then he took my hand and said "Son you are the decent and of the great warrior "Nogitsune Yagami" he was the great grandfather of your great grandfather."

He was the unbeatable and unsung hero of their era. He saved many people from the hands of the cruel The Harlots. Harlots were from the east and massacred the whole west valley within only three weeks they had a reinforcement of more than 500000

soldiers who were all well trained and weponised. They knew the art of Psychic power. Which helped them to take over anyone's mind and make them do whatever they want? On the way to reach this land they piled almost 10000 death bodies in the neighbor empire and burnt them without any hesitation! People started to call them the "Terror of the Nightmare."

Their main power-house was their leader "Mashira Saitan." He was so powerful that people used to call him "THE GHOST OF EAST." As people say he was able to control both fire and the power of some mythical beasts. One of them was the most powerful *Nine Tails*, and *Behemoth*. Whom he used to destroy the whole enemy alliance with an instance.

Here is the interesting part "Nogitsune Yagami"was the brewer of the mystical bird The Phoenix who was considerably the most powerful beast of all.

It was a huge bird with flames on its wings, and flames were coming out it's eyes and as a fact it was Immortal. And it was able to manipulate thunder and flames.

Saitan's main aim was to capture The Phoenix as it was way too much overpowered and getting control on it would have made him the most powerful being on this planet. But for this he has to defeat Nogistune. So he attacked the nation.

The war began and all the reinforcement of Saitan's army invaded our borders at once and for the purpose of protecting our people "King Issca" sent all the soldiers to the borderline but this was a wrong decision... All our forces shattered like house of cards as Behemoth was on a roll he killed and ate most of our soldiers alive.. And he was all alone not accompanied by The NineTalies.

It tensed the situation of the nation and King was almost on his knees ... Seeing this Nogistune was not able to hold back himself, so he went on his own and challenged Saitan for a one on one duel.

The day of duel came nearer and nearer but between these days the enemy keep on invading our nation and to stop it Nogistune went on a rampage along with Phoenix and masscared all the enemy reinforcement.

And the screams of those dead enemy forces are coming to your dreams and thoughts. They are just a reminder to you that you are the successor of the Great Nogistune

On the day of duel all you can see were dead bodies laying all over the barn land of East and can even smell blood in the air. And every single person of our nation was hoping for the best they were praying for Nogistune's win over Saitan and will save the country.

The duel started. And Saitan screamed out "Hey you there.... Nogistune!! I have been waiting for this for a long time..." the look on his face was full of excitement and evil.

It all started with a bang without wasting any single moment Saitan unleashed his fire powers. He attacked Nogistune with some heavy attacks which were really desvastating but because of luck he escaped all of them and was standing on his foot. It was Nogistune's turn he used his fighting skills and used his arrows to damage Saitan but he protected with magical barrier. Then Saitan just rushed towards Nogistune and kicked his chest.And then he used some of his powerful attacks on him which heavily injured him.

Nogistune's condition was not good. He was not in the situation for a fight against such powerful foe. Then he had his last hope Phoenix he called him out.

Seeing Phoenix out Saitan screamed with a laugh like he was only waiting for this to happen. At that instance Saitan call out both Behemoth and Nine Tails and this duel was going out of hands. 3 of the most powerful beasts in a single ground!!!!

The fight began as between the three most powerful beasts: Saitan and Nogistune begin!!

The fight was looking not well for the Phoenix because he was fighting with two beasts at a time. Phoenix barely able to defeat the Behemoth because Behemoth was injured during the last battle.

Nogistune see that Phoenix was having a hard time against Nine Tails. Nine tails used one of his most powerful against phoenix and it severely injured the phoenix. So Nogistune asked Phoenix to get away from this battle beacuse it was really imposable for

phoenix to win that battle. But phoenix came to him and asked Nogistune to take its all powers and ability but he said that "If i take all your powers you will die and I don't want my friend to die!!!"

But pheonix without saying any word gave al his powers to him and said "Here I am your friend by birth I have been by your side from the time you were born and for that I want to thank you. Take my powers and defeat this evil!! And Save your people"

The next moment Nogistune used hiss all powers and strength to attack nine Tails and he was successful in doing so he severally injured him and made it fall on the ground with the cost of his left hand.

Then he rushed towards Saitan and with all his remaining strength he attacked Saitan and like a bullet makes holes. He made a hole in the heart of Saitan. Then he said that strength...... Where ever you see shadows "*In this accursed world nothing goes as planned until and unless you put your all efforts and you will also find the existence of light*"

"And this is the reason of your nightmares. And as my experience says they will disappear now". Said the Old Monk.

The fight fought by your ancestor saved the kingdom. And gave the whole world a spiritual aspect of war as every war is not about kiling the humankind but some also look forward to save them. Be a savior not a the one to be saved. Be a damn WARROR!!

VIII

BIOG 8- ANAMIKA KUMARI

Philandering from a very weeny hamlet to steel megalopolis Jamshedpur wasn't tranquil for me and my kindred.My appa who is a government employee made me to grasp the delusion that he once deluced for himself.

Delucing to be fit in a white coat with stethoscope around the scruff for making the confraternity free from slow poisioning hurdle.So,here an ungraduate lassie "The Anamika" who just remains in her own world with lots of esstasy without showing any hurdle to others and become esstasy in bringing smile in

others face is going to make a path in she never tried off.

I inevitably believe in sedulous and for the best verdict that are yet to come and meet me.Without having much cognition in writing I tried my level best to instigate something quirky and promethean.Just crave to corcuscate like the Sun in the sky because moon also dissipate with the light of the sun.When I ecompass with inconsistent shades of colour and strains I relish my best juncture with myself . Every problems in my life edify me how to tweak myself more and how to bring positivity in negativity also.

RATAN TATA- THE INDIAN INDUSTRIALIST

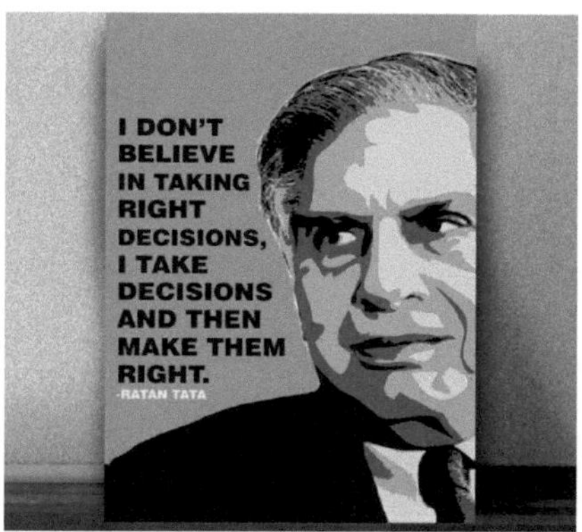

With a great nervousness sitting on the sofa made my heart skip some beats. Seeing the setup and the processing going on the set to start the interview I got a nervous breakdown.

"Ma'am, do you need some water?"- My assistant asked me.

"Yes, I need a glass of cold water" -I replied. She got me a glass of water and I felt little relaxed.

"Good luck, be prepared" -came a voice.

I turned my head back to see who it was.

Surprisingly it was the interviewer who was going to interview me.

"Are you nervous?" -He asked politely.

"Yes, not for the interview but for the conversation we will have that is on a great personality"- I mumbled anxiously.

"Alright then, let's start after 10 min"- The interviewer said.

The interview time arrived.

I and the interviewer got ready and sat opposite to each other.

He welcomed me and started the interview.

"What comes first on your mind when you hear Ratan Tata- The Indian Industrialist?" he started with the question.

I answered "Gold is always gold, it usually sparkles

A star on the sky always twinkles

Scratch on a diamond; never lay down its glitter

The great Tata Ratan with no filter"

"In short, his name represents who he is that is a RATAN. He is one of the greatest Indian Industrialists-"I added".

Hearing the above lines the interviewer gave me a wide smile.

I continued "Even after belonging from Tata family, he never enjoyed the luxurious life. From his childhood he believes in hard work. Believing in his thought, he started his first job of his carrier in the company of his father named TATA GROUPS OF

COMPANIES and later in 1991, he became the former chairman of TATA GROUP OF COMAPNIES. Moreover he also learned how to fly an airplane".

"Was he really following a simple life style?"- The interviewer enquired.

"He was very simple, as simple as his name. Just a tie with a short and blazer over it and a smile on his face makes his look completely. His determination towards his work and the way he handled the workers of such of a commercial enterprise industry shows the quality of his leadership. In his presence the revenue of the company increased by 40 times and the profit increased by 50 times last year. Apart from it, he is never proud of it. He had established over more than 100 companies in more than 100 countries in the world. Despite of these many achievements, his down to earth behavior is what that wins the heart of many people"- I replied proudly.

“So as per you, he made the industries stand on its feet?"- The interviewer continued his enquiry.

“Off course, he is the one who made the industry shine like a star, with the help of the workers"- I exclaimed!

Working with him as a manager, I witnessed what he had faced in his life. I had seen me carrying the burden of failures and even saw him reaching the enormous height of success.

"Had he ever seen failure in his life?"- The interviewer questioned.

"Why not! Even Albert Einstein had failed at some point of his life, then why do you expect that TATA had never failed, in his life"- I answered.

"If that's the case, then please share something about his failure".

"There was a time when he launched his dream car TATA INDICA in the market. But his expectation didn't touch the limits. The car brought many negative feedbacks, seeing this all the other members of the company asked him to sell it.

In order to sell it, he went to meet FORD. He encounters FORD and told about his loss in the company. Then FORD, disgraced TATA by taunting him that if you don't have expertise in car merchandise, then why do you squandered money for it and also told him that he was doing a favor by buying it"- I said in gloomy voice.

"But after hearing this, Tata committed to himself that he will make his company stand on his own feet and never let down his self- respect in front of anyone. So he returns without selling it. He worked, so much that within a few years he made his company stand again and also modifies TATA INDICA. And when FORD was in loss, at that current year TATA bought LAND ROVER and JAGUAR"- I said with a glow in my eyes.

"That means, don't take revenge from your opponent just make yourself so powerful that the opponent realizes not to mess with you again"- The interviewer exclaimed.

"Yes! And this is the one of the qualities of TATA which makes my soul to accept him as my ideal"- I said with pride all over.

"Then behind the success there must be some reasons"- interviewer enquired.

"You caught the correct point'.

He advises and he himself follows his three formulas to get success in life. ***That is-***

1. ***Inevitably treat yourself as- spesh and never let yourself down, because deity hadn't made anyone junky. So be yourself with your own thought.***
2. ***If we eschew our self from what others are implementing, then undoubtedly we will achieve the success at higher peak.***
3. ***Never expect from everyone that all will praise and will proud of you. Just make yourself that much capable that your parents should feel proud of you.***

"So this was his success and failure history, which motivates us and initiate something new within ourselves"- interviewer expressed his views.

Then he added " What about his personal life? Why didn't he get married.............?"

“That’s the good question. In an interview he had once said that he was in love with a girl in Los Angeles. But for some works, he had to come back to India. While going he made a promise to that girl that he would surely come back and would marry her. During his presence in India, her parents made the girl marriage with someone else. That broke him but he didn’t let it affect his carrier. But in memory of that girl for whom he promised not to marry anyone else. He remains bound with them"- I explained being little emotional.

“If someone ask me what is love? I will narrate his story to them"- The interviewer said with a smile.

“Have you ever thought what he would have done if you were in the place of success"- The interviewer questioned?

As I was about to answer his question, there was a power cut in the set due to which the set got dark and the conversation stops.

IX

BIOG 9- JYOTI RANJAN SAHOO

For a long-drawn-out temper, he concluded that there's only one scheme of la vie: And that is to be joyous. The inception and conception was obtuse. A few inception vow a commence that ought- to confiscate longevity to persuade a commencement. Prior to the basic fundamental locution bang the leaf, or the first

satisfactory and reasonable idea that come about, there is the tangled or complicated matter of breaking the silence. "Some throw up before they can breathe"- that's itself the enlightening light- Jyoti. Not all can run to the door at the knock of announcement- granted one hears it. Not all know what it means. Simply, not always is the gift of talent given free and clear- exclaimed the "SCGs". Some who are marvelously passionate to write may have to spend half their lives learning what their proper subject matter may be.

DISAPPEARANCE- THE NEAR

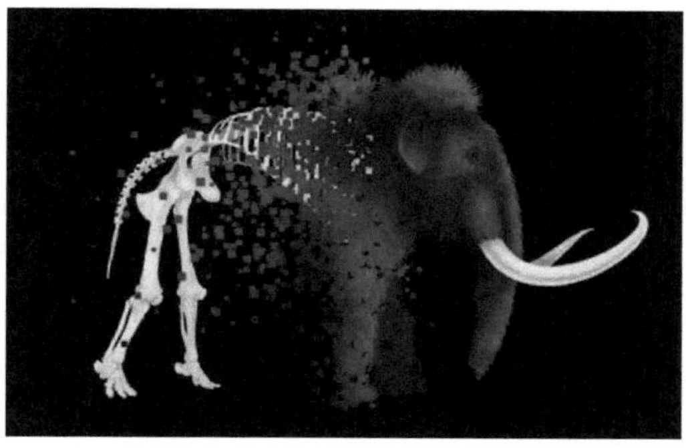

Oh good! This erection and fabrication exertion had made the twenty-four hours, the disguise.

Not even able to centralize the intellect on the studies. Arey! Ediot my exams are approaching! Please put a stop to the exertion work.

Nanu: What I can do homie? The new land proprietor is trimming the foliole and off-shot of the woodland.

Me: Why is he effecting so?

Nanu: Mr Lawr, is assembling a new galleria.

Me: Hun! What? For an arcade he is fragmenting 50 acres of land?

Nanu: Yup!

Me: I think Mr. Lawr don't know that the green land is an accommodation to a chiliad of beastie and critter.

Nanu: It's unfeasible and unimaginable. He is well cultured and accomplished.

Me: Oh! For you literary and refinement might be, getting a highest degree by appearing exams. No it's all about how you bring into play, the memorize and learn by heart facts and condition. Had you conceptualize, that what will ensue, when these creature will perish?

Nanu: Mind not! Nope

Me: It is because you are anticipating for the new plaza.

Get out of it!

Why are earthling homo sapiens blood thirsty?

And how do we vindicate deed of sheer in inhumanity.

Nanu: We are persisting and continuing our bread and butter and is able to upkeep because of "in-humanity", only.

Me: Wow! Shit man! Disappearance- The Near.

I had ne'er been to such a state of affairs. So substandard to shatter the woodland and it is even more amateurish to remain quietude upfront of this type of brutal and barbarous activities.

I grievously don't acknowledge what will eventuate in the upcoming procreated era.

In the eventide o'clock, while scrutinizing the "Le Monde"- a peculiar and uncanny reportage amazed me. The news was-

" Dear, Terra Firma, I had faded from the place where homo in-sapiens reside and inhabit". I the "Panthera Pardus Orientalis", oftenly called as- Amur Leopard.

Me: Pere, why personnes of the la terre are devastating the unharmed habitat?

Pere: Beta! It is a sway of anthropoid income. "That is- play havoc to live".

Me: But, Pere- what about them who are dashed by them. How can I make them au fait regard this?

Pere: Being an adolescent minor, you are earnestly answerable to it.

Me: But!! Pere..... !!

The slash- "You are answerable to it", didn't oblige me to snooze that particular isolated nuit. The solitary action that was forthcoming to my frontal lobe was- How can I put a stop over this? But I was lagging of ideas.

The next morning, during my peripatetic to the ecole by the footway, I detected- "the industrie" from which dangerous fumes and gas were impending out in a soaring mass. God! This tailback congestion and smokes around the ether are too noxious, that may demolish me now only- Exclaimed my Pere.

Yes Appa! Contamination, currently are improving by degrees day-by-day. Existence now has turn out to be a battle stations, where we the man-at-arms warriors are enterprising brazen audacious deed to get out of the battle.

Crap man! I am behind- schedule to the ecole today. What directrices will hypothesize. Don't agonize! He will not be indignant on you for sure. Bye appa! By by..

When I set foot in the ecole acreage, was still feeling infatuation for those jeopardized breeds.

Beens dias echolen. I miss G. Radhika your new "environmental impact analysis- ecology" pedagogue.

Student's: Good morning miss.............missssss

Nanu: Hooray! She is so appealing and attractive, looking like a salmon- pink coloured rose in a pink kimono.
La...la.laa..lla...laa... love at first sight.

Me: Hey Nanu! Focus on her teaching not on her mug and kimono.

Nanu: Why are you always tedious and dull.

G. Radhika- Hey scholar! What's going on there? Why are you gossiping? Consolidate here. One important topic is going on- Meters and sensors.

Me: Sorry miss.

G. Radhika- To measure the concentration of pollutants present in a closed environment, you can use an air pollution meter. This device tracks the amount of particulate matter (PM), formaldehyde and total volatile organic compounds (TVOC) present in the air around- prompted from the book.

Nanu: But mam, why homo sapiens soul are tainting and poisoning?

(The class continues and so on..)

During the evening time, In the course of twilight time, I arrive afterwards down by the companion way from my leg room and interrogated my mere that why was she so distressed.

X

BIOG 10- MONALISHA ROUTRAY

The world is full with great personalities, who had inspiring and motivational stories. By getting inspiration from them, a drowsy, unknown, unquestioned girl with great vision wants to create her own history. An undergraduate scholar- The Monalisha wants to recombine the unknown gene by crossing the

limits of failure. Gradually, what supposed to be in her dreams, now they all comes outside of the retina and stores in her encephalon. That drowsy girl now wants to do something unusual and something creative. A shiny, plainness, unpigmented coat with an auscultation in hand to serve people. She wants to remove the dark clouds and to bring coterie full of effervescence, tranquility and contentment. She is a girl who always used to be in a gambol and tantalizing grump with less inventiveness get necessitate into a completely new world full of sophistication, denizens and conceptualization. She always put herself in tint and the world with her besom. She had never envisaged herself to be in the world full of liberal arts.

ADOLESCENT PROBLEM

"Peep-peep "

"Peep-peep"

The busy vehicles honked through the metropolis. The sun gleamed red in the pink evening sky. It was the time for the students to return back home from their schools. My mind drove faster than my scooty that rushed in between the cycles and school vans.

My mind was lost in the files that were pending to be submitted to the boss.

Out of nowhere, a girl walks into my path with a bag, more like a hump.

Three of my fingers reach out to clutch on the break and my scooty stops with a jerk. Startled, I stand still, unable to process any words. A visible alarm could be sensed on her face. But she turned and walks away hurriedly. My eyes travelled to the brim of her skirt with a red blood.

My mind drives back to the 15 years old me.

I belonged to an Orthodox family with not so modern mindset. My father worked as a teacher in a small town, who was strict about my education.

On a pleasant morning, with a noisy sound of cock, I woke up early in the morning and found all the things were being packed inside cartons. I asked my mother the reason behind it, so she told about the transfer letter of my father and within some hours, we needed to leave the house.

I didn't have the idea that, we were moving to a modern society. Through the glass of the car, I was able to see the clear-cut view of the contemporary world. Sparkling of light and smoky environment just created a confusing thought inside me. Actually I was very exhilarated to see a new world.

On the very next morning, I woke up in a nervous manner- that was the first day of my school. By holding the four fingers of my father, I stepped forward into my new journey. I smiled as my eyes landed on the towering building which seemed to touch the sky, but as my eyeballs moved towards the ground, my smile faltered.

I saw a group of girls standing at a distance; a sudden thought struck my intellect, "Wow! What an elegant and attractive physique", they all seemed senior to me. But that was just for a while, I entered into the classroom and it didn't take much time to alter my thoughts. "Are they really my classmates?" I questioned myself. An unusual nervousness crept up my mind. "Would they accept me as a friend?" I glanced at myself. My smile dropped and I walked away silently.On the next day of my school, when I entered into my classroom, someone threw a crumpled paper at me. When I picked it up and opened "A HIPPO", it read. Someone from the crowd repeated the words and everyone started laughing at me. My heart raced and a red tint of embarrassment appeared on my cheeks. It was really awkward. Ashamed, I walked into the class. After that incident, when I finally calmed myself down, a group of girls came towards me, "How oily and sticky your hair is" one girl spoke out.

"Why are you wearing a dress, come with a saree. That will suit you better." One of them pulled my hair and threw my ribbon away. I panicked. Uncontrollable hot streams ran down my cheeks. I just ran away from the classroom and sat under a tree, which stood at the last corner of the playground.

That day, I didn't attend the classes and ran away to my home.
My mother asked, "Vani, what happened?"
I just looked down and kept crying. After some time, in a crying and panicked voice, I questioned" why only me?"
"Why am I different from others!" my voice trembled. I started explaining what happened at the school.
She put her hand on my shoulder and said "All these are normal".
" Just try to change yourself and be friends with them."

I looked at my mother and left without another word, I never expected those statements from her. Repeatedly one question struck my mind, "why do I need to change myself?"
"Can't I remain as the person I am?"
I tried to ignore all those things.

Next day morning in the school, when I was just moving towards the classroom, a group of girls passed by me but one of them hit me by her shoulder. I lost my balance and fell down on the floor;

one of my shoes flew away from my foot. Some of the girls took it and kicked it around like a football.

I ran here and there desperately, trying to get back my shoes. Yet, they paid no heed.

One of them threw it into a drain and walked away nonchalantly. I stood there for an hour, totally helpless. Nothing came into my mind, I was completely blank.

Regardless I attended the class with one shoe only. Everyone teased me all there day. Gradually the day ended, not looking at anybody else but the ground I was slowly walking down the stairs. Suddenly I heard whispers behind me, I looked back and saw that some of my classmates were laughing while staring at me. I was totally confused, after walking some way I felt odd and un- comfortable, turning back I got a glimpse of blood stains at the border of my uniform.

Anxious and uncertain about what to do next, I ran into a dark alley, where no one was supposed to go. I sat there with my mind filled with several questions.

"Why I am so fat?"

"Why Am I ugly?"

"Is it a sin to be ugly?"

"Is it entirely my fault?"

I wiped out my tears and walked towards my house, that day I was really late to my house. I opened the door quietly and got into my room. The night was totally filled with darkness. Yet the darkness of my shadowed mind was unmatched. I was lost in the dense sky. No tears could explain my emotions. I decided that I would give some modification to my body to be attractive.

I googled about the methods to become more beautiful. I got an idea about the diet pills. Without thinking much, I decided to buy them. So, I secretly bought it. Keeping it a secret from others, I started continuing taking the pills daily.

Day by day I became thinner, weaker and paler. My total decision proved to be wrong. Gradually my face was covered with pimples and I became uglier than before. I was also getting afraid about what would happen with me next. My parents also questioned what was happening to me and how I was getting weaker.

The problem got added up rather than being solved. My situation was too worse, that I couldn't even step out of my house. I locked myself from the eyes of the society. I was ashamed to move out, my parents decided to take me to a doctor.

After consulting the doctor, he took my situation into consideration and prescribed me some medicines.

Even my results went down gradually. Teachers' impression towards me got depleted. I was pressurized by my parents too. Weared out from the entire situation, I went to my bedroom.

The cramp seemed as painful as my worries. Amidst all these thoughts, I plopped down on my bed due to a sudden cramp.

“Will this ever change?" I wondered.

XI

BIOG 11- NANDAN KUMAR ROUT

While I was skimming noble-

Abruptly cruor in the capillaries initiated sinuous and soul started fluttering as the phone. A notification from the wisdom of the aspiration pressurizes the mind and pervades it with euphoria. A notification came from the Sambad, the tranquility, tried to stir my captivity with sensibility. It was drifted there "Nandan" you banged "JEE ADVANCED" and you are tabbed from

IIT BOMBAY at rank 3000.

Hurry, feeling proud going to be an IIT-Ian one who can't do an effortless problem, then over a time, now with eventual depravation from the cerebrum to the head will give him the success which can't be forgotten in his lifespan. Reality is that he is not a gamer. He is a voracious reader but sometimes the black circle of his eyes made his mind towards "gaming".

"E- LEARNING"- TODAY'S PLATFORM

" Education is not just about to going to school and getting a degree.

It's about widening your knowledge and absorbing the truth about life." - SHAKUNTALA DEVI

Now a days the world has come to an extreme point, that nothing impossible with digital media.

There were two friends "Roony" and "Jasmin" they belong to Los Angelis. They both are friends they know about each other's secrets feeling and thoughts effortlessly.

Roony found a strange thing inside an old house. The house was of his fore father. When he opened that strange thing he was shocked by the things that he saw inside box. He asked Jasmin

about her knowledge about this strange things, but she denied it was also new for her also, then he asked to his father, but his father said that he don't have any particular idea on that thing and referred to ask his grandfather, he may know. They went do the grandfather.

When they reached to their grandfather after looking the thing got shocked and happy. After seeing the smile on the grandfather face both Roony and Jasmin asked, why you are happy. Grandfather replied it has been ages seeing the "Book" in this century.

After hearing the word book grandfather laughed a bit and explains to both to the children's. Grandfather said it is filled with mixed letter forming words which were not moving at all line it does in our screen.

They got excited about hearing the definition of the book and full excitement say "WOW!" The name mentioned on the book is "The journey of the plague year 2020", written by -Anurag both Ronny and Jasmin ask "Why 2020 is plague year ?". Then grandfather said it long brief story with real circumstances and world filled with grief and fear of virus. After hear my explanation of the grandfather both by them, became excited to known about the story behind 2020 plague.

Grandfather said when I was 15 year old. It was bright Sunny day and travelling with my friend to school with happy and funny moments is we are our school first batch and classes started from 10:00 AM classes are enclosed with four walls and interaction between the student and teacher and teacher explaining briefly new concept to us in interesting way, in the lunch break we enjoy the midday meal with our friends and without restriction we are sharing our food with each other. In the time between 3.00 PM to

4.00 PM we are having our physical activity after end our school we went to our respective home. After some month finally the Annual Exam student, in the last secondary exam a notice came from Central Government. "The school will close for 10 days" due to increasing of Covid-19 case".

In the mid of the story Roony and Jasmin ask what is Covid-19 virus? Then grandfather said please have some patience. Now I will continue the story.

After hearing the holidays from the Central Government the student ignore the Covid-19 and made the holiday as a vacation and move to the tourists place. After a week again a notice come that the holiday extended for a month due to large amount of Covid-19 cases. On hearing this I and my friends started to gather information about Covid-19 pandemic and we realize that this disease can risk our life. The Covid-19 origin come from fish market of "WUMAN" the country of Chine, the virus is airborne and contact diseases which spread though out the world, we circulated to the school game and spread the awareness about the Covid-19 who celebrating the vacation and roaming through the world without any caution about apprising pandemic. At the 25 March 2020 declare that from that day onward next twenty day's. It will be complete lockdown of the country due to the wares situation of the Covid-19 virus. Day by day increases of Covid-19 cases the Central Government decided to not to open the school and collages rather start online virtual classes until the Covid-19 cases decreases gradually.

A bulletin came from the schools and colleges, virtual classes will start after week thoroughly zooms or Google meets application. It was a first time through the virtual classes as I was abide worried and excited about the classes in the new platform. There is no one to disturb my study and I can concentrated in more on the studies as there is no one to irritating. In the virtual classes the teachers make the topics more attractive and interesting about learning them and we can study or ask doubt regarding the topic for 24 x 7 hours. At a period virtual education as a peak point.

(Voice of mother)

"Roony and Jasmin time for the Snacks" said by mother. Grandfather said, go children have your snacks we will end the story here.

Granpa- Granpa !! Hear something we want to tell you about how was the lifestyle now a day we have a specific room, which is extremely technical.

It is include everything that a student of them day need. At your time education was I between four-wall and now, it has become so much of school of the school modified that you can learn everything by being any where you want, any time you prefers it is up to you. E-learning does not limit only to the learning of the school syllabus but also to various competitive exams which can press as pillars for the jobs. The inability of the teachers to guide us 24 x 7 is solved by the handy technology. Our skill does nil remain bounded to the people around us but can reach to the whole world through internet platform. When the traffic due to transport of students has reduced, making the roads a little less crowded. The use of fossil fuels is. Saved due to this, helping the sustainably of the environment. The big universities like the oxford require graters resources for admission but similar lectures can now be accessed through the facilities of e-learning.

In my point-

> E-learning is very affordable & it is available for everyone.

> "If E-learning's used wisely then it is fruit full but if it's not used currently then you will regret it throughout your life."

“"E-learning is changing and we will see new models,

new techno & design emerge.

So, let's drop the "e" - or at least give it a new and wider definition".”

- Elliot Masie

XII

BIOG 12- NISHANT MAJHI

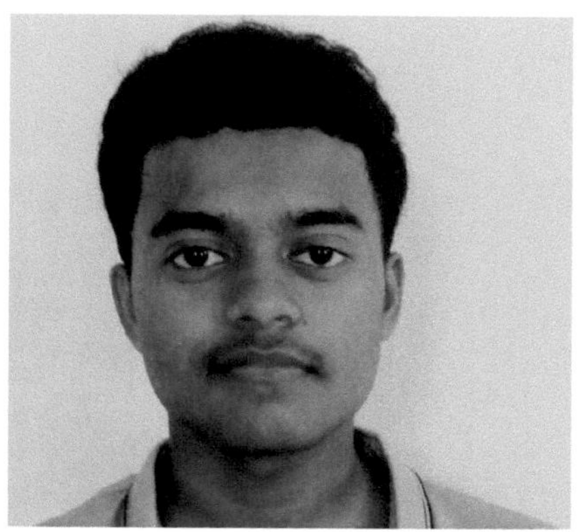

Sun is bigger and brighter, but it never had captivated the atypical one as the moon does. Some kichi no hito generally ask, why don't you try making vignette? But the real rejoinder is never been mentioned that,"fine feathers make fine birds." And the fine feathers are the "astonishing" which is extraordinary or unreal. Customary doesn't interest him even the slightest.The normies of

Sri Chaitanya oftenly mention, why are you always silent? And it was always an indefinable henji "because I hate drama"Examining thoroughly everywhere, as far as the slight can reach and finally put breaks on steps to an unknown world "Anime", swiping the way of thinking about existence, to the world of fantasy, mystery, ecchi, slice of life.The gliterified combination of mixed words and pictures formulated "Manga", made a deep impact in the inner space of the bosom that picturesque a new hustle "NISHANT".

GREEN INDIA- THE FUTURE 2047

It is a chilly night of a hot sunny day. I successfully concurred on another boring day, where I'm surround by shelfish people, who will only remember me when they are in need & eventually forgot me when the work is completes "the world of fakes". The thing in that I just want a friend who is not "Fake" like the whole world is.

"CHEEZZ!!??" a creepy sound of some machine & a beam of light came to my back for some second.

I was shocked & turned to my back.

"Who's there?" I shouted,

A boy of 18-19 years has fallen on the ground, as soon as I saw him I rushed to the boy, in the intention of helping him.

When I reached near him, I saw some unusual clothes & a very technical watch wore by him. Ignoring all this abnormal things, I call an ambulance & take him to the hospital.

"He is all fine now, I think he accidently touched an electric wire", said the doctor.

I don't know what actually happening, but I somehow feel relief after knowing that he is alive. I don't know who this guy is but I kind of feel that I'm related to him somehow.

"Aeehm??" the person makes sound, I got excited when I saw him opening his eyes.

"Hey! How are you felling?" I asked with a smile, I'm not that much talkative but I still asked him. I don't know why?

"Good I think" said normally, the guy without any expression said,

"What's you name & where are you from?" asked curiously.

"My name is NISH & I'm from the ... ahem, I don't know where I came from? And who are you? And why these people with while coats have surrounded me?" said sportingly, this guy know his name but don't know where he came from... that's rather unusual.

"I think this young man has lost his memories in that electric shock, as time will pass he would eventually regain his members", said the doctor seriously, I don't know what should I do ?

"If you don't have anywhere else to go, would you like to come my home" I asked happily all this is not something I say to anyone!! I don't want anyone in my home; I just hate other people crawling in my place. This is not me at all, who has possessed my body? And all above this person is not a girl either so why am I feeling related to him??

"Yes why not !!, I will come to your place", said laughingly, that is not the reply that anyone give to someone, at least try to say no at first then say yes but this guy without any hesitation want to came along with me. Just who is this guy anyway?

"Yes! That would be great, we don't how to arrange any bed at this time of the day, and can I sleep now". Doctor said, what the heck is going on? This doctor also doesn't want to keep this guy and saving his ass he put all the works on me, where the coat of justice has gone? Am I being prank right now? But I don't see any cameras tough.

I don't know how I ended up living with this guy under the same roof. Yaa! I actually know I was the one who invited him to stay with me; I still don't know why I do that? What so ever.

"Don't you remember anything?" asked thought fully. I think there could be something that this guy was hiding in front of that dump- ass doctor.

"Yes my name is NISH", said with a smile.

"Yaa Yaa ! Except that?"

"Not at all!!" said seriously, is this guy for real?

I just met this guy and he has started irritating me! I just want to hold his necks for some minute...... heehaw!!

"MMM... how much it the rent of your house?" asked with not much expression.

"Rs-15,000 -monthly" I said proudly.

"HUU?? That's cheep!!" said with a nasty look, just what this guy is thinking ?? Cheep?? Don't he knows price of tomato is Rs. 75+ per kg now a days, price of everything is increasing day by day, and all of that, he is saying my palace in cheep, just give me his neck, my wall are been decorated with quotes & filled with anime figurines, the room that a otaku prefers.

"If you don't like coming here, you can just leave," said with a rude look, why did I bring him anyway?

"Yoh!! I was just kidding, actually I like your home quit much, it's walls are filled with famous anime quotes, Manga & anime series shelf & most of the characters figurines, this place is so cool. I always wished to live in such place. Thank you so much to invite me here", said happily, MMM, I think this guy is not that bad and helping others who are in need is a part of humanity naa..... mmm.

"Yah, Yah, not a big deal you can live here how long you want", said with smile.

"Thank you so much, aren't your parent coming home?" asked thinkingly.

"No! I'm living alone for my studies; my real home is long ways from here. Anyways you hungry?" said normally.

"Ohh ! So that's why your room looks like that mmm."

"Yes! I'm", said excitedly.

"So what you like to eat?" asked gently.

"Pizza!"

"That's not something that you eat at late 3.00 AM."

"Chicken kaabab ?"

"No!"

"Saahi biriyani?"

"Ok, I'm cooking something myself if you want you can join me".

"You are so boring!!" said with not so good look.

"The door isn't locked yet! You can leave now also"

"Yoh ! Don't be so mean ... cook something I will try my best to finish it, Ok !" said slowly.

"Ya Ya whatever! I'm heading to kitchen now; I will make some noodles in my royal way".

"MMMH, it smell good"- said curiously.

"The royal noodles, only thing that can be cooked by me!" I smile proudly.

"I'm starting!!" said loudly.

"Ok, go on".

As he ate the noodles, tears started coming out of his eyes. I didn't said anything to him, maybe he have remembered something from his parents. After that I arranged a futon for him & we slept.

"Rise & shine dummy! It's morning already" shouted out loud,

"Aah my eyes!! You forsaken witch you won't get away easily", he said while sleeping. Ignoring whatever he may be saying, I pulled out his blanket and take him out of the house. I gave him some of my clothes to wear.

He always suggests going to 5 star restaurants but he doesn't know the taste of dhaaba...

"Hey! One think I asked to forget", he said with a serious look.

"What?"

"I don't know you name yet".

"Huu?? I think you are living with me from last night and it is middle of the next day and you still, don't know my name, Whatever- it's HIKI" said irritatingly.

"Ooh..." he murmured, He was kind of looking shocked by knowing my name. I don't know the reason why?

After all this, we carry on outing. I was on my summer breaks & I can do whatever I want. As time passed by, we kind of became close friends. We got for outings on daily basis; we go to cafes, parks, karaoke and much more. Our favorite place was that Dhaaba. We share so many things in common and I can say he is not "FAKE" the whole world is filled with. This is the only person I enjoy living with.

Days later, we are on our outing again, visiting our favorite Dhaaba.

"Shooff !!" he pulled me back in the corner & he look for someone on the way.

"Yoh! Bro something came upon me... would you please head back to home?" said seriously.

"Yes! But why? What happened anything that I can help?" asked seriously.

"Na... Na! You don't have to worry about me, if you want to do something for me you can cook your Royal noodles for me... but please go to home now", he said seriously.

"Ok ...whatever, I'm heading home; the dishes are on you so come back earlier"

"Yoh!, good bye & take care" he shouted with a big smile.

"Hmm, bye!" confused.

I don't know what I going on in his mind. I reached home cooked my special Royal noodles, so much time passed... NISH is not coming back. He have to wash the dishes, where is he? I'm bored; I'm watching some anime on my TV now. (Changing channel).

"A boy of 18-19 year has found dead, near Gulmohor Dhaaba, there are some unusual laser burning marks are on his body, if you know this person please contact us". (Television)

Tears came out of my eyes. I'm shocked, I don't know what should I do, what going on I can't believe. I changed the channels but everywhere the same news was there that a boy is found dead! I don't want to believe what is going on. Is this the play of God?

"Zizzz-Zizzz..." his watch vibrated, when it touched it a hologram of him projected in front of me.

"Yoh! How are you? You would be good oblivious. If you are watching this hologram, so that means I'm dead by now. There was so much thing that I want to say when I was alive but the right time never came so I'm starting now. I came from the future of years 2047, There is war going on in our time because the resources of India are not kept in good, the corrupt Govt. indulged everyone into war, many and many people are dying. The Green India campaign, which was started to increase the number of trees due to climate change. Those number of tree were sold to other country & the resources have decreased to high extend and you in the future became weapon specialist and made some decisions that shouldn't be taken which started chaos among states then counties and I have came here to stop you from doing all this. Hey dummy, where are you? Yoh ! You are calling me in the past; I have to go now thanks you so much for what you have done for me. Save the world and become the hero but don't forgot to meet in the future & when you do that let me know by saying I have saved the world, Tata & take care"

The hologram stopped, I cried so much, the only person I consider as my friend is no more with me now, He is a liar to, he said he would come back & it my royal noodles and now he is not coming. Why things like this always happen to me?

When I went to take corps of my friend in the hospital, I found that someone has already taken his body as his relatives.

Later I found that some people from feature where finding him and for saving me he sent me to home and go for fighting with them and was killed by them, by the weapons that I have made in the future.

Knowing what is going to happen in the upcoming future, I tried to change myself. In this world of "FAKE" try to be the real one, be the original of yourself not the first copy, do good and stay silent because good things are not done to get someone attention, but to give aid someone who is incapable now I worked hard day and night to make the world war free which was the late wish of my dearest friend.

As time passes by in the year 2025, I completed my studies and started my research to increase Greenery in the world, with a girl who is my friend and it is not like we are in any relationship or anything it is that we are just friends.

In the year 2027 we have made test of our portions and I also end up marrying that girl, I don't know how? It is what just it is ... He he.

In the year 2028, our experiments are failing drastically there is nothing we are able to do now.

In year 2029, our time is not better yet but we haven't loose hopes... work is on, is between this harsh time my wife gave a present of becoming a "Father", Now how harsh the time will come we are not letting our hopes down.

In year 2036, it is 7th birthday of our son... Our work is now all good and now we have to show it to the whole world.

In year 2041, I get approval from the Govt. to use my product whole over India.

In year 2045, more and more people have joined us & our product is being used whole over the world.

In year 2047, it is the 18th birthday of my son & I told him "I have saved the world".

XIII

BIOG 13- ADITYA SAHOO

The drops of rain coming from the roof , making a beautified harmony that can lead one to a peace of mind. The miraculous combination of vocal or instrument in a pleasing manner that always gives joy to my heart, takes me to another world where I can be myself "ADITYA", who likes to listen to the delightful voice

of the nature. Strings of sitar , the notes of piano makes his reminisce his good times. He understand everything better than anyone else. Aditya , more than a son ; sun to his parents. Brilliantly hospitable to fresher's but the funkiest one, once you start knowing him. His eyes hold a dream of wearing the apron and the stethoscope. The one who have the least senses. His heart remains in the lap of his friends. This lazy lad tends to be the most dynamic and vibrant fellow. Basically being an "All in one" package. A hamper full of snacks or a delicious lunch invitation would be the best present you can surprise him with.

EXTRATERRESTRIAL LIFE- THE ALIENS

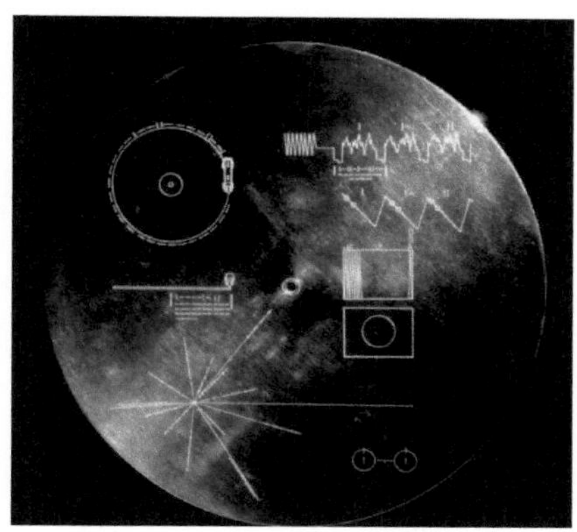

BY NASA:-"HELLO... Can you hear me?"

Srikant:-"Yes, I am here; I have a great surprise for you."

NASA:-"ok, we are here waiting for you eagerly."

Srikant:-"Ok......"

(After a while)

"Are you there; Can you hear me?" (No response from the astronaut)

"Sir, the spacecraft has already blasted and destroyed upon the equator of earth over the region of Washington for which we are not getting any signal from Srikant."

After Investigation...........

"Sir, we have found some of the evidences but we don't have any clue whether Srikant is alive or not."

"What evidences?"

"Not much. Just a suitcase which is already half burned."

"Immediately bring it to me."

Open it safely this suitcase can also harm to us, as we don't know that is inside it.

They senior officer opened the suitcase and found a diary.

(Now the senior officers opened the diary)

Hello my best friend, today I got my result and I have only got 60% .After seeing my mark, my mom replied that it is all because of your aimless life. I was crying and gone upstairs, and sat on the roof top thinking about myself that what I will do in the future?.

Suddenly, a shooting star with great lightning passing through the city, I was very surprised to know from where it came? Mother came with the supper and asked what your aim is? I replied I had to become an ASTRONAUT. From that time in started a new journey of my life.

The very next day I started gathering information about space. Then after I completed my elementary education with 92.65%.

Then for higher studies I left for New Delhi.

Finally after 2 years, I qualified for IIT and decided to pursue a degree in aeronautical engineering. Then I work hard to fulfill my dreams.

Then I completed my 4 years course. I finally joined ISRO. After working there for several months, I transferred to NASA. That was a very joyful moment for me and my family also.

After gaining adequate experience the senior officers had selected me for the mission to MARS.

After completing all the prior formalities and all my trainings. Finally I was prepared for the take off.

When I was ready to go to space I checked twice if anything I left or taken already. I was fine to go to space. My team members calling me, "Sir, let's go," It was a feeling when, "the dream comes true". My eyes were filled with emotions and heart with full dedication.

I put forwarded my 1st step in the stairs of the spaceship. That was the moment when my foot step was not on the earth surface for 5 minutes! And my blood vessels was flowing towards down.

I was quite furious and can feel my heart beats. And within seconds the rocket left the earth surface and fly to air.

After a short period of time, I saw we have already reached into the space, "It's time to wear the space suit and carrying the oxygen cylinder" said our officer "Yes I'm ready".

After spending several months in the spaceship we finally stepped on the MARS. They roamed around the surface searching for evidences for aliens but no such evidences could be found in the first 11 days.

One fine day, while my crewmen were resting I was trying to fix the recorder on my space helmet. Suddenly I experienced some inhuman sensation.

(At Present)

"Sir! I found a microchip."

"Have you checked it?" Sir asked.

"Not yet sir."

So, hurry up!! There could be any information about Srikant or else about the aliens.

(Microchip played)

Suddenly after listening the sensation or a drastic sound, I came out from my ship and started investigating the condition of ship. While I was investigating, I suddenly lost my sense.

When I opened my eyes, I found myself in a closed dark chamber where nothing was visible to me and I was surrounded by some unseen creatures.

Then they took me to a place which was full of lights and I was able to see everything with the face of the unseen creatures, who were taking me.

They took me to an anonymous area where I astonished by seeing the different types of gadgets, which I have never seen before and I was very much scared by them, the only thought was revolving in my mind that "how can I get away from this place otherwise they will kill me".

After spending several days,

I came to know that there is no way to escape from here and I lost my hope of living. Suddenly the creatures came to me and opened the chamber in which they put me for several days and they took me to their lab for researching me. They fitted a gadget on my head and the boss sat in front of me. I thought that they are trying to harm me but they were trying to talk with me by the gadget fitted on my head.

They asked me some questions such as "Why you came here and what the reason is?" I answered them "we are not here to harm you or to destroy your kingdom."

"How can we believe you? Is there any evidence?"

"As you can see I don't posses any weapons on me!"

"No, we don't believe in you"

The boss said me in a deep voice, "We will turn you into an alien."

I am very scared of it and at that time they opened the gadget which was fitted on my head and again they put me in the closed chamber.

After a while, they gave me an injection which will clear my brain, I suddenly lost my sense and I was not feeling well but suddenly a creature came close to me with another injection, I just got more scared but the creature opened the chamber and said to me, I am here to help you(in our voice) .

"I got shocked by this. And asked how?"

The creature replied me i will give the antidote and will help you to escape from here. At that time I was so much happy and also scared.

He gave me the antidote and told all the secretes of the creatures called "ALIENS".

This continues for 10-15 days and the day came for which I was waiting for because on this day the aliens go for hibernation to increase the kingdom.

And the time came, they all gone for hibernation and only the creature who helped me left. He gave me all the information we gathered in 15 days and finally he show me the way for escaping the mysterious world. I requested him to come with me but he denied. So I left there in their spaceship.

At the time I reached mars, my crewmembers shocked by seeing me alive.

They cured me and ready the ship for launch to my own world.

(Micrhchip stopped)

(At Present)

All the members of the NASA clapped for it. And they transferred all the data of the aliens to the all Space centers.

This gave a view to the future generations that "Homo-sapiens are not only be the only creature existing in this universe. In the era of new world there will be a less captivation of human beings as compared to this new creatures" so called as "ALIENS".

XIV

BIOG 14- NIHARIKA PRADHAN

"Passerine are those, who soar up but they never pinion down tranquillity"

I belong to Dale where floret burgeon out of the Garth by tearing the pages of hanker but I wouldn't. The pages of triumph were

only witnessed by the one who is into it with a passion of winning. My heart presume the path to triumph is always filled with hurdle but our aim is to ignore the hurdle and focus on our goals because the lustre of success is incomparable with any other things in this entire world.Surveil the miracle ensuing in the nature is something which allure my scrutiny a lot. It is quiet unusual that how a fruitful lives for a day where as slowpoke lives for 150 epoch these little variation in nature fascinate me. The blithe moment for NIHARIKA is when she follows the throb of music, which is the equilibrium state for her.

MOTHER NATURE AT HER BEST

The sun seemed brighter, the grass was greener, where I laid under the shade of a mango tree and just near by a river flowed, whose water glazed and shimmered under the sun. The flower at the river bank seemed to dance. The smell of the grass and the flowers filled the atmosphere with redolence. Everything was just perfect but suddenly I noticed something wrongs the water in the river turned black, the flowers withered, the mangoes in the tree rot and it's leaves started falling, the grasses turned yellow and but sun grew brighter and brighter. I stood there astonished, and then I noticed a beautiful flower from a far which wasn't destroyed. It seemed as if the only hope, I ran towards it without any delay but.... But a strange sound pricked my ears, I felt as if they were crying that sound made me terrified.

But then I found myself in a beautiful bed room the very next moment, soon I realized that it was a dream or nightmare I can say.

The strange sound which I heard was the ringing of the alarm clock. I stopped the alarm clock and went near the glass window of my room and opened it. It was for the first time that I did so, because my room was air conditioned.

The dream made me feel restless. I looked out of the window of the 27th floor. Buildings, buildings and buildings was all that I could see. It made me quite disappointed.

"Aarya ! Aarya ! Freshen up and come down stairs for breakfast", I heard my mom calling.

Then suddenly I remembered that I have practical exams at collage. I hurriedly got freshed up, wore my uniform, and went to down stairs, "I don't have enough time to sit and take breakfast" I told to my mom loudly, then picking up one sandwich from the plate, I ran towards the car which was waiting outside the house. I was in deep thoughts even while sitting in the car.

"You are here ma'am" The driver's words interrupted my thoughts.

"Oh! Did we arrive at the college?" I said.

The sandwich was still in my hands; I gulped it in a one go and went inside the college.

The lectures started but I couldn't concentrate on what the professor was teaching. All I could do is think about the nightmare I saw.......

Is it really going to happen? Will the nature get destroyed as it happened in my dream? Many question arrived in my mind.

Then the next day, there was a notice on the bulletin board at collage, that a few students were selected to be volunteers and go to several uneducated place to spread awareness about Covid-19 and cleanliness. There were three groups and one group was given under my lead. All the three groups were asked to select one of the uneducated places they wanted to go. My team selected a small village named Kosala.

I went back home and informed my parents about the awareness program. They agreed to let me go.

"Pack all the necessary item which might be useful for you there" said my father in a deep voice.

Mr. Anuj Tiwari, my father is a well known industrialist of our city, who rarely have time to sit and take food, What he does is only his work, work and work! I packed all the necessary items required for the journey.

"Aarya ! Aarya !" I heard the voice of my mom.

"Come downstairs and have the dinner", she said I went down to the dining hall; the atmosphere was filled with smell of delicious food, and sweets.

"Mom did you prepare all there?"- I enquired.

"Yes Beta, all your favorites", she replied.

I went near her and gave her a tight hug and kissed on her cheeks and said, "Thank you Mom, You are the best".

Finally came the day when we had to leave for Kosola, we all got on the bus with our luggage and helped Prabhati Ma'am, our guide with her luggage.

"All of you tie your seat belts to be safe, the bus is about to start", commanded Prabhati ma'am.

We all tied our seat belts and the bus started.

We played some music and enjoyed all along the way. I felt a little drowsy so I slept. The howl of students woke me up; they were shouting and hooting because we had already entered the village, Kosala.

I raised the curtains and glanced outside the window.

"Oh! That's so wonderful!" I exclaimed. Greenery is what, I saw all around, it was my first time to have seen such a large field with green trees, because I grew up watching concrete buildings, malls, factory's, industries and nothing else.

Finally the bus stopped.

"Students take your luggage and go down", instructed our guide.

As a leader, she asked me to lead the troop and check that every one settled in their rooms. The place where we would stay these days was a small, old but a long house with ten rooms.

We booked seven rooms, one room for Prabhati Ma'am and three students per room in the rest six rooms.

The moment I stepped down from the bus, I felt as if I have never seen the world.

I always thought that the world is made up of concrete but that's not it.

The world has other sides.

The cool breeze, the smell of the soil when it's about to rain and the surrounding with trees all around made me feel mesmerized.

Every one settled down in their rooms and had some snacks which we took along with us. Suddenly it started raining there; I was so excited to feel the rain so closely because my mom never allows me to go out in rain. But today I would do so. I ran out of the guest house and started dancing the rain. Looking at how I enjoyed it other students also joined me. We danced joyfully and had much fun. But out of luck Prabhati ma'am didn't notice us doing so, or else we would have been dead. All of us caught cold due to getting wet in the rain.

The care taker of that place came to know about it and so She prepared a medicine out of Tulsi, honey, gingers, black pepper etc and gave us to drink at first we hesitated but eventually drank it.

To our surprise all of us were cured the next morning.

"Aunty, how did you know that this medicine wills were us?" I questioned to the care taker.

"It's an Ayurvedic way to were cold", she replied with a smile.

"That's amazing!" I exclaimed.

"Can you say me a little more about Ayurveda", I added.

"Sure why not?" She said

"Ayurveda is a way of curing diseases naturally and without much expert expense, Nature takes care of us just as mother does for her child" she added.

"Oh! Wow that means nature has the solution for every problem as my mom closed! Am I right aunty?" I said excitedly.

"Yes Beta,but now I have some work to do, I will talk to you later".

Saying this she went outside the room.

Later we went out for the awareness program, while we were out, I encountered my new things.

We went to several hours of the village for survey and came to know about many things such as people of the village used biogas for looking. They planted many trees in their garden. People there, were self dependant and hardworking but still they had enough time for their family. The atmosphere there was so calm and fresh that I barely wanted to leave.

Finally, the day came when we had to leave the place and go back to our city we bid farewell to everyone and placed our entire

luggage in the bus.

Then I ran towards the caretaker aunty and gave her a tight hug.

"Good bye Aarya!" She said in gentle voice.

Tears rolled down my cheeks "Good bye Aunty", I'll "miss you" I said gloomily and got up on the bus. Then everyone along with Prabhati Ma'am settled down on their seats and the bus left for the city.

After reaching home, I shared my experience to all my friends. They all were amazed and envied me.

On the evening when I came home, Papa was sitting on the couch with a laptop and working on some documents. I went near him and sat next to him, he turned his face towards me and gave a smile and said, "How was your experience there?" "All Good papa", I said

"Can we do something which the pollution can be reduced? Because our factory emits a lot of pollution which harm the nature", I added.

Listening to this he seemed quite happy and promised me to use lead free petrol in the industry which will reduce pollution quite a lot". When nature is treating us like her children then we should respect her as a mother. The efforts that Mother Nature gives for us are incomparable.

Sri Saichaitanya Global School, is the brain child of National Integrated Caring Education Trust.

MESSAGE FROM THE DIRECTOR

we have achieved a lots of milestones and helped thousands of successful student in launching their career. All the time, we are putting our best efforts to bring the best to the students. Sri Chaitanya has built hundreds of success stories and helped students to achieve their goals since its inception.

OUR MISSION

Our mission is to prepare students to be fully equipped with all knowledge in our fast-paced changing society. We will also lead in educating students about diversity that will enable them to better understand our differences, to unite and respect each other. We will ensure that our students develop their skills and intellectual competencies that are essential for success and leadership in the future. To bring change in quality education of weaker, deprived and vulnerable students and to make them scholars through participatory education and for their welfare development programs.

OUR VISION

Our vision is to develop confident, responsible and well mannered students who aspire to achieve their full potential. We will do this by providing a diverse, secured, fun and supportive learning environment in which everyone is equal and all achievements are celebrated.

A Page Of Response And Views, If Any

Printed by Libri Plureos GmbH in Hamburg,
Germany